DEDICATION

To my wonderful grandchildren:

Elizabeth, Thomas, Michael, Stevie, Angelica, Christofer, and Joseph.

May they always be strong and healthy!

Note To Parents

It amazes me how much children absorb, they look at you with that innocent face and know exactly what you are saying and sometimes thinking even before they learn to talk.

I believe if a child is introduced to food according to what it does for their body, they will look at food differently. They will become aware of what the food does for them, not just the taste. When a child decides he or she wants to run as fast as his friends he will remember the story and think - I will have some milk to make my bones stronger and some protein for energy - and that is the beginning of associating food with well being for the rest of their lives.

I would like to share with you a couple of stories of how we tried to introduce healthy food to our grandchildren. Our four year old, Michael, was told that spinach was good for his bones. One day he fell and hurt his head really bad and went crying to his mother, "Get the spinach I broke my head!!" We just have to make sure we tell them it has to go in their tummy to work

I do not have many sweets or as we say junk food in my house. I personally try to eat healthy and have an apple everyday. One day I only had one left and my grandson asked if he could have it. He saw the struggle in my face because, it was my mid morning snack and I was looking forward to it. So I said we will share it, he was thrilled and has asked for an apple every time I am with him. He is a teenager now and I still bring him an apple.

This book was written for five year olds and under but one day I was discussing it with my daughter at dinner and my nine year old grandson piped up and said "So what do these string beans do for me Grandma?" His comment is indicative of what food does regardless of age.

Mommy! What do carrots do?

Carrots help you to see things **better.** You can see far away,

the clouds,
the moon,
the sun and tree,
your Mommy & Daddy,
friends,
sister & brother.

Mommy, what does spinach do?

Spinach gives you muscles
so you can play and pick up
big balls and toys

.and give
strong
hugs to

the people

you
Love!

What will a Hamburger do?

Hamburgers have protein and will make you grow tall and run fast.

You can
reach things
in
high
places.

And what if I drink ALOT of milk?

You will have a bright *smile*.

You will have
STRONG
bones to
jump

and climb,

or jump a rope.

What does Cereal do?

Cereal helps you go potty and helps your tummy feel better.

It helps you play games on

the computer.

What will an Apple do?

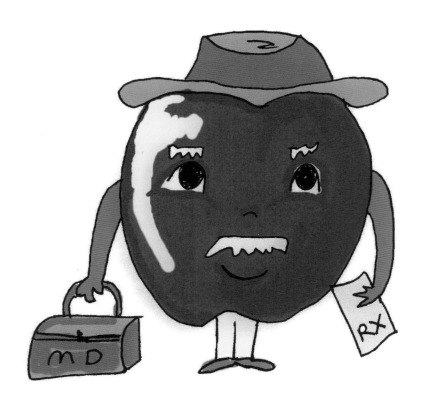

An Apple a day will keep the Doctor away.

Apples help keep you
healthy

and help you think!

You can learn
to count and
do your ABC's.

What will Fish do?

Fish is brain food, it
makes you smart

And Quick at

Puzzles

and Word Games.

What does Water do?

Drinking Water keeps
you from getting dizzy & tired.

When you run

and play,

it keeps your body
running too.

FOOD PYRAMID

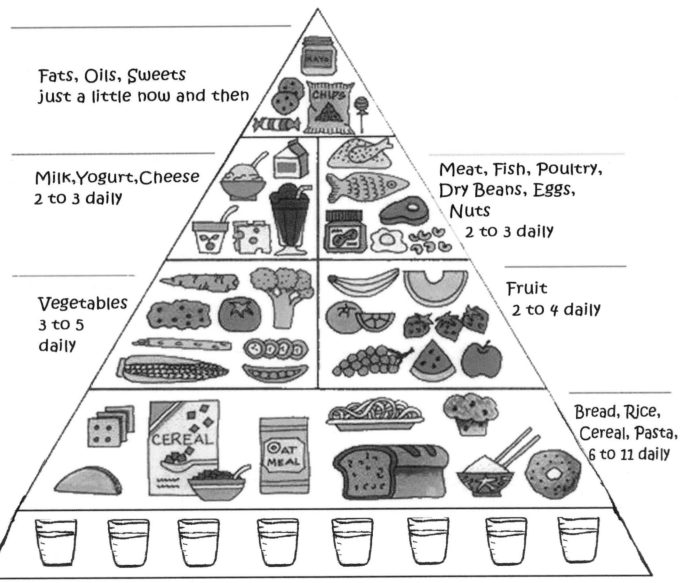

Fats, Oils, Sweets
just a little now and then

Milk, Yogurt, Cheese
2 to 3 daily

Meat, Fish, Poultry,
Dry Beans, Eggs,
Nuts
2 to 3 daily

Vegetables
3 to 5
daily

Fruit
2 to 4 daily

Bread, Rice,
Cereal, Pasta,
6 to 11 daily

Water- 8 Full Glasses everyday

Made in the USA
Lexington, KY
09 December 2009